SOOTHE THY SOUL
YOU ARE WOMAN

I dedicate this book to all the women out there and the men who love them selflessly.

I am grateful for the special ladies in my life; my mother (Fidelia Obaseki), my sister (Isoken Obaseki) and my other wonderful ladies.

I respect and cherish the selfless men in my life; my husband (Emmanuel Briggs), my dad (Chris Obaseki), my brothers and wonderful fathers, husbands and brothers out there.

What's your version of the definition of who you are? You are exceptional, but you must choose to embrace that.

EHIMWENMA VALERIE OBASEKI

I LOVE THAT I AM YOU

Dear woman,

I love that I am you,
that I feel your pain.

I wish we learned
that unity helps us survive.
I hope we finally realize that our battles are similar.

If we choose to accept the truth right in front of us,
we will embrace the life we were made to live.

To cheer one another;
to hold on to love, faith, and harmony.

I wish we learned that a lady's tears could be ours;
that we have to find some means to survive this life.

Dear lady, I am you, you are me.

Dear grown woman,

I had my first view of you as a child,
through my mama.
However, I never understood the life of a woman.

How could we be ungrateful?

They say we learn more from experience.
Now I am her;
though young, I see her in my every move.

13

15

YOU COMPETE TO BREAK

Dear woman,

I wonder why half the time you compete.
It is a battle of who is stronger, who is wiser;
who is more of a superwoman and super mother.

Dear woman, do you realize that when you do this;
you silence the others?
What about their challenges?
What about their lost pain and healed misery?

Do you think their efforts are nothing compared to yours?
You take the crown but keep a heart broken.
You silence the words of a woman in need.

She can't speak up because
her problems are supposedly smaller than yours.

Dear woman, we compete to break.
We support to mend.

We can all be exceptional together.

19

SCARRED TO UNITE

Dear woman,

Scars seem to be a prominent part of our existence.
However, what makes your scars even more unique is;

Your scars bring life.
Your scars cause existence.
Your scars are beautiful.

Your scars are evidence of memories past.
Your scars are the source of your life force.
Your scars cause limitless stars.

Your scars mold you into the person you were meant to be.
Each life we see today,
is a product of a woman's scar.
Without these scars, there'll be no life here.

We are scarred to make and unite.

YOU ARE ALTOGETHER BEAUTIFUL

24

You are altogether beautiful, my darling; there is no flaw in you. (Songs of Sol. 4:7)

Dear woman,
How dare you make yourself an object of ridicule!
If he told you that sex was all you had to offer;
did you ask of his mum?
Or his sisters?

I can assure you that he has sisters who have dreams.
I bet he respects his mum.

Did you remind him that you are 'woman'?
A proud one.

How dare you look beneath yourself
and feel the impact of his words!

You do not even owe him an explanation.
He is the product of a woman.

You are beautiful!
Don't you forget that!
However, what's most important is:
You are a woman of substance;
not to be toyed with.

Be you and be a proud WOMAN!

27

GIFTED WITH LOVE

Dear woman,

When I was younger;
I judged you a lot.
I judged your choices
I judged your actions
It wasn't deliberate.
I was quite ignorant.

I thought life was either white or black.
I didn't understand that it was gray most of the times.

I never saw beyond the emotions of a woman;
understanding our need to be loved and cherished.

I asked, "why express such emotions over little things?"
But giving is the life of a woman;
loving is the life of a woman.

They say "she's a fool for loving him that way."

Now I understand that,
it takes deliberate strength to say I can do this no more.
It takes a struggle for us to refuse to give love.

Now I am older;
I am a mother, wife, sister and friend.
I understand better.

31

YOU ARE WISE AND SUPPORTIVE

"When she speaks, her words are wise, and she gives instructions with kindness."
Proverbs 31:26

Dear woman,

We all know we need one another to survive.
We all know we need to take each other's hand and strengthen one another.

What if the hand we take hurts us so bad?
What if that hand takes us to future doom?
What if the mouth of the person who holds you is deceptive?

We can still thrive and pray for her.
Nonetheless, we must remember we are on a journey;
A journey to succeed and bring positivity.

Sitting maliciously and discussing vain things won't take us there.
Dear woman, choose your friends, choose your words.

35

YOU ARE POWERFUL

Dear woman,
 As I sat in our last gathering;
I noticed something,
you were quiet and withdrawn.

You seemed intimidated because she walked in.
I am not sure how well you know her
or what they said to you.

Maybe they said she is more beautiful than you.
They said she has the class and carriage.

Woman, be you; do you.
You do not owe it to anyone to redefine your person.
All that counts in your action is;
your person is bringing about positivity.

"She is energetic and strong, a hard worker."
Proverbs 31:17

SOOTHE THY SOUL: YOU ARE WOMAN

Dear woman,

I called you in for a meeting
because I could see your smart and endearing nature.
You showed me all you worked on.

I was surprised to see that you did all that while taking up
a very tasking job.
You worked nine to five.
Then you had the kids and your husband to take care of.
I also noticed that the chores were endless.

When you showed me your projects,
I was in awe.
I termed you a 'superwoman.

I was perplexed when you refused my offer.
You were made to be great;
I noticed you were scared to be great.

You were scared to be greater.
You feared that your success
would make your husband feel less and intimidated.

Do you remember the vows you made with your husband?
He promised to love you.
I don't think he will be threatened if that love is real.

If he's a real man,
he will want your success
because your success is his success too.

If he's a real man,
he will be your greatest cheerleader.
Love is supposed to be beautiful.

Dear woman,
your home should be built on two people who choose to
succeed together.
You can also be great.

Dear woman,
I got the news,
I heard a miracle passed through you,
you gave birth.

I once witnessed a life miracle,
It was breath-taking.
While I sat and stared at my miracle,
I wondered how a person could come through me.
I felt honored.

I wanted to congratulate you,
when I went on the media and saw your post.
You discussed your experience.

I also read the comments;
other women started arguing that,
they had it worse.

Someone said you were lucky because you had a C-
section,
another lady attacked her and said she was lucky
because she didn't have to be opened up.

It was disheartening; those ladies who bore such miracles
could try to hate on each other and compete.
They missed the point.
They failed to realize that they were all superwomen.

Dear women, the pain we went through and the joy that
came after is everything.
We were chosen!
Let us hug our sisters.
We are all powerful.

42

Dear woman,
*   The other day, you went in for a program with a friend.*
You were in a society where women are looked upon as
second-class citizens.

You spoke, but you were ignored;
His voice was more of a valid one to them.

It is astounding how many brilliant ladies we have in this
world.
So smart, independent and endearing.

Refuse to be silenced at any point in time.
Your voice matters.
Your intellectual ability isn't gender-based!
You are insightful.
Your point is valid!

45

YOU ARE A TEACHER

Dear woman,

Your little girl walked in and asked you a question;
you dismissed her so quickly.

She asked about 'sex'.
She is twelve years of age.

Don't you think it's time you spoke to her?
There is nothing to be shy about.
Let me tell you;
If you don't teach her,
someone else will!

You must learn to embrace the fact
that she is growing into a beautiful young woman;
a person with feelings and active hormones.

If she feels intimidated and uninformed,
You will be hearing more about her from someone else.

She is a curious soul;
her curiosity is going to be fed.

Dear woman,
  Why do I see you teach your child the same thing
you preach against with your husband.

Somehow, you are exhausted at his inability
 to help out with chores.
You ask; "am I a maid?"
Then I see you teach your sons to frustrate someone else',
daughter.

Please be fair.

YOUR TIME IS NOW

53

Dear woman,
I lost my grandma.
I couldn't stop thinking about her.
How much of her life did she feel was a passing phase?

I saw her pictures when she was young and beautiful.
I wondered when she withered to old age.
Then I asked, "what can beauty products truly do?"

I noticed; the beauty products don't take away the reality
of things.
They might succeed in reducing.
It never truly takes old age away and the internal feeling.

I also know they can't make the organs function like that of
a youth...

Grandma withered like the flowers...
She's gone.

Time does exist woman.
You live life once, please do it all now.

Dear woman,
Society tells you what to do and what not to do.
Why?
I mean if a man can be scolded for the same offense you
might have committed, then maybe it's okay.

However, if a wrongdoing excuses the man.
Then that's a double standard.

Don't get me wrong,
I am all for living right,
and doing the right thing.

I strongly believe
wrongdoing isn't gender-based.

59

YOUR CHOICES DON'T BREAK HOMES

Dear woman,

I saw how your so-called victory was celebrated
with your friends the other day.
I heard you say "he finally proposed."

I was about to rejoice with you
when I heard you say,
"I taught his wife a lesson."
Then you said; he is now yours.

Mama taught me to be kind,
I can't help but wish you all you wished her....

How dare you rejoice in her pain!
How dare fight so hard to frustrate a fellow sister?
I know her husband had a part to play
but you rejoiced.

I have something to say to you.
He is not yours.
He belonged to someone else.

You broke a potentially beautiful thing.
I hope you realize someday
that love isn't always rosy.
I hope you feel the pain.
I hope you see the truth.

I am sure you will silently realize your wrongdoing.

63

YOU ARE WISE

She speaks with wisdom,
  and faithful instruction is on her tongue.
Proverbs 31:26

The time was still.
In the circle of cheerful youths.
Laughter was a confused expression of youthful freedom...
Where no much sorrow resided

As we slid through time,
Each passing day had a snapshot.
A Snapshot of history...
What we all could be...

The taste in their mouth turned sour.
No more ignorant laughter.
But thoughts of survival and freedom.

Some left behind,
With a circle no more...

Dear young woman,

It is amazing to be a single youth.
You find diverse opportunities.

I hope you find the right one.
I have something to tell you:

As we all grow, our life and plans will change.
Our priorities will change.

I have one wish for you;
that you don't regret life
because you made decisions too early.

I had a friend,
who at one point, felt like she had everything.

She had the so-called 'coolest' crew.
She had all the boys drooling over her.
She thought that was all that mattered.

It might have been too early for that.
She let her guards down,
and started to drown.

YOU KNOW WHEN YOU ARE READY`

Dear woman,

Love is great,
the ability to share it with someone is impressive.
You get to build your lives together,
raise kids and share a beautiful, purposeful union.

I want to remind you,
not to forget your dreams and aspirations.
Remember your goals before you got married?

I know you have to adjust and create room for each other,
but please don't forget your dream for a better future.
Love your kids and your husband but don't put a hold on
your future.

I know sometimes we have to take breaks;
due to immediate circumstances.
You know when you are ready.

Dear woman,
You looked on social media the other day,
it appeared like all your friends were getting married.

You questioned yourself and asked;
"why am I not getting anyone?"

There is a time and season for everyone.
Your friends are not better than you because they got
married.
Everyone has a different story to tell.
Everyone is running a different race.
Your race is different from mine.

I will also like to remind you that social media love is no
love.
It is unreal.
Everyone tends to show you the good side.

We all have our silent struggles,
so keep living your life,
keep being you.

Keep facing your dreams,
the one deserving will show up on your way to your
destiny.

75

YOUR HOME IS BLESSED

A wife of noble character who can find? She is worth far more than rubies.
Proverbs 31:10

Dear woman,

Love is beautiful.
What makes it even better is, two imperfect people
coming together to complement one another.

Jimmy Evans once said "if you think the grass is greener
on the other side,
you need to water your yard."

I know it is great to have our support system to share
things with,
however, let us remember that if we need real solutions,
we might have to take a different route.

It is a more active step; we slowly water our garden,
to make love flourish.
Stay persistent.
Keep fighting for love,
never give up,
communicate, and pray.

Keep praying; keep loving.
Leave the rest for God.
He will show up for you.

"Blessed is she who believed that the Lord would fulfill His promises to her."
  Luke 1:45

DO NOT AWAKEN PREMATURE LOVE

Daughters of Jerusalem, I charge you
by the gazelles and by the does of the field:
Do not arouse or awaken love
until it so desires.
Songs of Solomon 2:7

Dear young woman,

I know peer pressure does exist,
I remember the university days when,
some will tell me it is necessary to date for 'experience'...

I don't think dating for experience counts.
I don't think dating because of plain attraction counts either.

I know we live just once,
however, we need to think a bit more before getting into a relationship.

It is incredible that even after careful consideration,
relationship struggles are inevitable.

A relationship can indeed break you for good.
It requires a lot of mental and emotional strength;
because love takes over.
If it's your first,
you kind of stay hooked.

"She is clothed with strength and dignity, and she laughs without fear of the future."
Proverbs 31:25

Dear woman,
* I leave you with these six poems.*
Hoping the words leave you with a soothing feel.
Hoping, you learn how to love and fight for each other.
Hoping the words, give you strength to keep fighting.
Hoping you find joy, love, fulfillment, satisfaction,
but most importantly PEACE OF MIND...
I love you, my woman.

SHE IS HERSELF

She builds herself,
works on her future and vision;
making it so unique by reflecting the light of her gain on
the world.

She learns from her mistakes;
chooses her path carefully.

Speaks with words of kindness;
leaves a mark on the world.

She is HERSELF.....
She accepts her name and Identity,
and decides to make something out of it.

89

SHE IS MAMA...

I see your eyes;
they showeth love.
Your embrace is warm.

In your sight, I find tomorrow's hope.
Dignity layeth in your heart.
Your memories are tender.
I feel your humble love.

Mama, I'm a mama.
I love that I give love.
How did you do it all these years?

You are my sunshine on rainy days.
I find hope in existence because you live in my world.

I love you.
Queen of my heart.

Dear mama, I love you.... Dear mama... You are W.O.M.A.N...

SHE IS WARM HEARTED

She holds me tightly,
and cures the loss.

In every pain,
she speaks lightly,
and realizes there are no limits...

My boundaries are her beginnings
She tends to my tender spirit,
and feeds my curious soul.

In her eyes; I see the light,
she brings my image to perfection with just a stare.

SHE IS A FRAGRANCE OF PEACE

She ignites this spark.
So rare
and her fragrance so soothing...

She carefully holds my anxiety in her rare basket,
to help me dismiss it.
Her voice resides in my reality for a lifetime.
She sees through the depth of my craft.
Pins my smile to her favor,
and wipes my unnecessary tears...

SHE IS PATIENT

There is no image of my perfection in her physical reality.
Her soul knows the right music of my dreams.
Then she holds me and never let's go.
Keeps me alive with her breathtaking essence.
She's exceptional!
Hey WOMAN, I'd rather be you!

SHE IS CONFIDENT

She walks in a room;
takes over the silence.

When she speaks,
she radiates a rare gift to humanity.

She takes on the task of a week in a day,
and makes it look so small.

She has no idea;
even her silence speaks CONFIDENCE...

99

SHE IS SUPER-PHENOMENAL

I AM WOMAN; I CHOSE TO EMBRACE THAT!
A PROUD WOMAN...
A SUPER-PHENOMENAL WOMAN

You made all the delicate, inner parts of my body
and knit me together in my mother's womb.
Thank you for making me so wonderfully complex!
Psalm 139:13-16

Ehimwenma Valerie Obaseki is an exceptional and creative writer. She started writing very early in her elementary school days; being inspired by her environment and prior experiences.
She believes she can use her write-ups to heal souls and inspire people to be better.

Website: www.ehiobaseki.com
Email: ehi@ehiobaseki.com
Twitter, Instagram & Facebook: @ehivalerieob